Woodcarving for Beginners

Detail of Fig. 40.

Woodcarving for Beginners

Charles Graveney

Studio Vista

337, 754/736·4

General Editors Janey O'Riordan and Brenda Herbert
© Charles Graveney 1967
Reprinted 1969, 1971, 1973, 1974
Published in Great Britain by Studio Vista
Cassell and Collier Macmillan Publishers Limited
35 Red Lion Square, London WC1R 4SG
Set in Folio Grotesque 8 and 9 pt
Printed and bound in the Netherlands
by Grafische Industrie Haarlem B.V.
ISBN 0 289 37008 6

Contents

Cover illustration:
Dolphin in Sweet Chestnut.

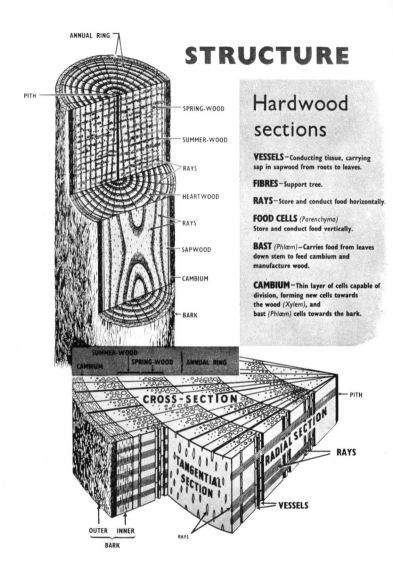

STRUCTURE

Hardwood sections

VESSELS – Conducting tissue, carrying sap in sapwood from roots to leaves.

FIBRES – Support tree.

RAYS – Store and conduct food horizontally.

FOOD CELLS *(Parenchyma)* Store and conduct food vertically.

BAST *(Phloem)* – Carries food from leaves down stem to feed cambium and manufacture wood.

CAMBIUM – Thin layer of cells capable of division, forming new cells towards the wood *(Xylem)*, and bast *(Phloem)* cells towards the bark.

Fig. 1 The growth of a tree. (By courtesy of the Timber Research and Development Association, and Educational Productions Ltd.)

Introduction

There is always a fascination in being able to make something, whether it serves a utilitarian purpose or fulfils an aesthetic or emotional need, and wood in its infinite variety, being clean and readily obtainable, has always been a universal material for satisfying these demands.

In early civilisations man had to fashion his own tools, grow his own food, make weapons to hunt with, build a house for shelter and furniture for comfort, and the skill acquired in making and working with such tools was used to enrich these simple necessities. They became not only utilitarian, but pleasurable to use and to contemplate.

In Saxon times the woodworker or carpenter was described as a builder of houses and maker of bowls, but carving as a form of self-expression became lost when the carpenter's work was subdivided into so many other trades: sawyer, wood machinist, joiner, cabinet maker, chair maker, architectural carver, furniture carver, polisher, and even sandpaperer.

So it is in the present age, with methods of production being broken down into so many detailed operations that no one individual is entirely responsible for the finished work. Also, the particular operation that he is concerned with is often so restricted in character that it is not sufficient to satisfy his needs, capabilities or talents. He may never see the finished product, and in many cases may not even know what it is. Fortunately the hours spent in this sort of production of what are deemed necessities are becoming shorter, and this spare time can be used to give greater scope for freedom of self-expression. Can it be just a coincidence that the anagram of talent is latent?

In the following chapters I have outlined a method of approach to an occupation that has brought satisfaction and pleasure to many people over many centuries. Although intended for beginners, it is reasonable to suppose that not everyone will begin with equal qualifications. Some may have experience in woodworking, others in drawing, design and modelling, all useful assets to the art of woodcarving, in as much as they train the powers of observation and stimulate the desire to produce in some tangible form a permanent record of a personal discovery or experience.

In reading the text it may seem that there are more problems than pleasures, but the difficulties will disappear as the practical work progresses, and with the increase in skill the pleasure and satisfaction in the final product will become much greater. It is important to enjoy the work, for it shows in the final result.

Many of the works illustrated are by students from all age groups. The historical examples show just a few of many applications of carving, some crude, others skilful, but all honest statements by artists who obviously took pleasure in the execution of their work.

1 Wood: its growth and qualities

A little knowledge about the growth of trees, why wood will split in one direction and not another, and what causes the decorative figuring, can be very helpful when designing for woodcarving. Whether the work is in relief or in the round, it enables one to select the best position in the wood, and to utilise the grain structure as part of, or complimentary to, the design.

It is necessary therefore to know what grain pattern will result by cutting in a certain direction, and by observing the cross section of a tree trunk it is possible to follow its life history. In the centre is the pith. This is where the tree started life as a young sapling, and as it grew each year in diameter as well as height, a new layer was added round the circumference. These are the 'annual rings' and are clearly seen as concentric circles extending right out to the bark; each ring consists of a light and dark band, the lighter one indicating the spring growth and the darker and harder one the summer and autumn growth.

The bark acts as a protection against pests, and inside this is a thin layer or sheath known as the cambium layer; it is here that the growth takes place when the sap rises in the spring. Radiating from the centre to the bark are lines or cells called medullary rays: these are not always sharply defined, but they are very strong in oak and beech and account for their decorative figuring. About two thirds of the diameter of the section is noticeably darker in colour: this is the heart wood of the tree through which the sap has ceased to rise, and is the most useful part as timber. The rest of the outer portion is sap wood which is still occupied in supplying nourishment to the tree; when felled, this part will take longer to season.

We are familiar with the expression 'to go against the grain', which suggests an opposing force, and grain is certainly the most important factor to be reckoned with, controlling as it does the design of every kind of woodwork.

It can be visualised as tightly packed bundles of fibres, some hard, some soft, running vertically the full length of the tree, and the art of splitting wood is not difficult, being the action of separating these fibres. The tool acts as a wedge forcing them apart, and the direction of split is controlled by the grain and not the tool. Cutting across the grain, however, compresses the fibres and increases the resistance of the tool, which in this case controls the direction of the cut. The only way to master the grain is to practice carving with all types of tools in all kinds of wood.

The pattern of grain is decided by the method of sawing or converting the tree into planks. This is done soon after the tree is felled in order to accelerate the seasoning process by exposing as large an area as possible to the air.

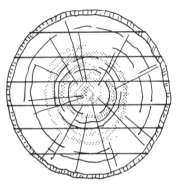

plain sawn

The three most common methods of conversion are plain slab sawing or through and through, tangential sawing and quarter sawn. The first is the cheapest and most economical, although it does not provide good figuring.
It is formed by making parallel cuts across the full width of the log, and the outer planks, being composed mainly of sap wood, are liable to warp badly.

b   tangential sawn

Tangential sawing, where the log is first trimmed to a square bulk and then planks cut from each side tangentially to the annual rings which gradually reduce in width towards the centre, produces a balanced grain pattern suitable for panelling.

The third method, quarter sawn, although more expensive owing to a greater proportion of waste, shows off the grain to the best advantage and is less liable to warping, as the majority of the cuts are radial.

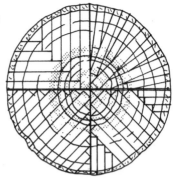

quarter sawn

Fig. 2 (a, b, c) Methods of converting timber.

Almost all woods can be carved with sharp tools, although naturally some are not sufficiently rewarding for the labour involved. Today a great variety of timber is imported from all parts of the world, many with strange sounding names. Certain woods have been fashionable in different periods of history, due no doubt to their availability. The hard woods grow mostly in tropical countries, and further north of the equator the timber becomes softer, finishing with the great pine and fir forests on the edge of the arctic circle.

Oak has always been popular for building and for furniture from the Middle Ages to the present time, although the once great forests of Europe are now very thin.

Walnut was used extensively in Italy, France and Spain during the Renaissance, and in Scandinavia pine still maintains its popularity for building and furniture.

When the sea routes were opened up by merchants, mahogany was imported into Europe and became the most fashionable wood for furniture from the seventeenth to the nineteenth century.

Many fruit trees are suitable for carving, in particular pear, with its firm close texture. Mulberry and lemon were used extensively by the Greeks and Romans, together with other varieties in use today: ash, beech, cedar, ebony, oak, walnut and willow.

The following list of woods is a guide to their quality and suitability for carving.

Afrormosia Golden brown with a green tinge, good figuring. Hard, carves well, comfortable to handle, popular for furniture.

Apple Pink, close grained, no marking, must be well seasoned.

Beech Pink to yellow, decorative markings, very hard close grain, good for smooth polished finishing of tableware, does not splinter.

Birch Yellow to brown, decorative markings, also suitable for tableware, spoons, dishes and plates.

Boxwood Creamy yellow and even colour, no definite markings, very hard close grain, suitable for fine detail, rarely found in large sizes.

Cedar Many varieties, deep pink to red, often with lighter streaks, very decorative, slightly perfumed, soft to cut.

Cherry Pink to yellow, hard close grain, needs to be polished to bring out decorative markings.

Chestnut, (Sweet) Pale golden brown, resembles oak in appearance. Although much softer, carves easily and no odour, good for bowls, can be brittle, sharp tools essential.

Ebony Jet black with occasional brown streaks, very hard close grain, fine detail possible, suitable for a brilliant polish, good to the touch.

Elm Yellow with strong dark grain, very decorative, can be very hard to carve, very durable, suitable for tableware, does not splinter, good for large sculpture.

Fir Red to yellow with strong, dark, hard lines, suitable for decorative effects, soft.

Holly White, close grain, hard, good for small detail.

Iroko Mustard yellow, tends to darken, similar to teak but much coarser, splits easily, not recommended for carving.

Jelutong White even grain, no marking, soft yet firm texture, will polish well.

Laurel Brown to green, close grained, cuts well, suitable for high polish.

Lignum Vitae Dark green with brown streaks, the hardest and heaviest of woods, close grain yet good to carve, has a slightly greasy nature, does not split easily, accepts a high polish.

Lime Light yellow, close grain, no markings, can be brittle, liable to attack by worm, strong, cuts well, obtainable in large sizes.

Mahogany Red, many variations of colour and density,

carves well. The two main types are Cuban or Spanish mahogany, which is very dark and hard, and Honduras, which is lighter and softer. Mahogany polishes well if given a tooled finish or if sandpapered, and some African varieties have a curly twisted grain that looks attractive when polished, but more care and sharp tools in the carving are needed.

Oak Golden yellow, darkens with age, English variety hardest, with most interesting figuring, good for exterior or interior work, architectural or furniture, very durable, needs bold treatment, most effective with all tool cuts showing, takes wax polish well. Austrian and Japanese varieties are softer, plainer and inclined to be dry and stringy.

Padouk Dark red, black streaks, very decorative grain, polishes well.

Pear Pink to yellow, very close grain, no markings but occasional dark streaks, suitable for small detail and figure work, carves well.

Pine Many varieties, including fir and deal, colour ranges from white to red, some with hard dark annual rings of resinous nature. Yellow pine turns pink on exposure to air. Soft, even grain, no markings, carves crisply, used for gilt mirror frames and furniture.

Rosewood So called because many varieties have a rose perfume. Red to purple with black streaks, highly decorative, similar to padouk, very hard close grain, will take a high polish.

Sycamore Ivory to white, very delicate mottled markings, close grain, hard, smooth silky finish, good for tableware.

Teak Light to dark brown, with dark streaks, fairly hard, close straight grain, greasy and gritty, carves easily, but will quickly blunt tools. Teak weathers well, is good for furniture, and has an odour that makes it unsuitable for food or tableware, polishes well.

Walnut Rich brown and often beautifully figured, very durable, close grain, excellent to carve. English, Italian and French varieties are lighter than the American or black walnut, which has a deeper colour but not such a decorative figure. Walnut is amenable to all makes of polish, and ideal for furniture or figure work.

Willow White and yellow with dark streaks near the heart, light in weight but tough and durable, easily bruised, cuts well with sharp tools, similar in appearance to sycamore, can be polished to an almost transparent surface finish.

Yew Golden brown, hard close grain, attractive markings, very durable.

2 Tools and equipment

The sight of a chart illustrating the great range of shapes and sizes of woodcarving tools must be very confusing to a beginner, and even to someone who has had some experience of woodwork and is familiar with a chisel and perhaps a gouge.

Basically, however, that is all carving tools are: chisels and gouges, mostly gouges, the majority of which have a straight shaft (fig. 3). These are suitable for most types of carving in low relief, chip carving, furniture, plates, dishes, and carving in the round, in soft and hard woods, where the tool is held at a comfortable working angle of approximately fifteen degrees to the work.

If the carving is in high relief, with deep recesses and undercuts as in much architectural and church carving, where dark shadows are necessary for the design to be legible at a distance, or on carved bowls, where it is not possible to cut deeply with a straight gouge, there are two other types of tool made to overcome these difficulties. These are the curved gouge or salmon bend (fig. 3h), and the bent gouge or spoon bit (fig. 3f). They can be used at a steeper angle to the work, from about thirty to forty five degrees, enabling the deeper recesses to be reached without damaging the surface carving. Another variation of the straight chisel or gouge is the type with a tapering shaft, known as a spade tool, of which there are three types. They are the short taper or fish tail, the medium taper or long pod spade, and the long taper, long spade, or allongee, as some manufacturers call it (fig. 3k, l, m).

The smaller sizes of these tools are lighter in weight than straight gouges, and they are intended mainly for use in soft woods and for the finishing stages of carving. The shorter tapers particularly are not designed to withstand heavy blows from a mallet into hard wood; some carvers refer to them as their Grinling Gibbons tools, due to their suitability for undercutting, a feature of the work of Gibbons (1648-1721), who was one of the finest woodcarvers who ever lived.

There are two further shapes of tool that are indispensable, the fluter or veiner (fig. 3e), and the parting tool or V tool (fig. 3j). The fluter has a 'U' shaped section similar to a

Fig. 3 Types of carving tools: (a) straight chisel (b) corner chisel (c) bent chisel, or grounder (d) straight gouge (e) fluter or veiner (f) bent gouge (g) back bent gouge (h) curved or salmon bend (j) V tool or parting tool (k) fish tail (l) medium taper (m) long taper.

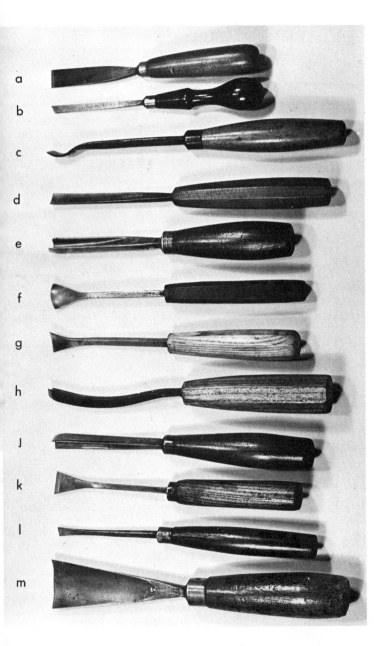

a

b

c

d

e

f

g

h

J

k

l

m

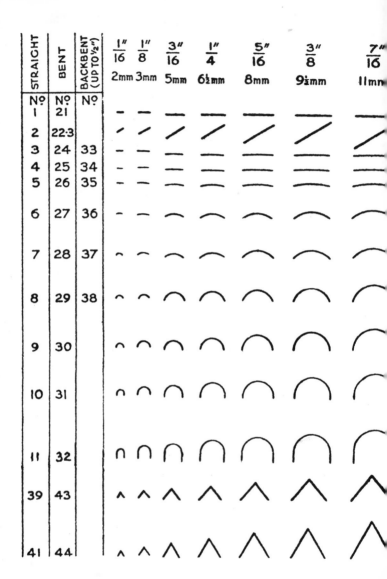

Fig. 4 Full size diagram of tool sections. (Courtesy Tiranti.)

16

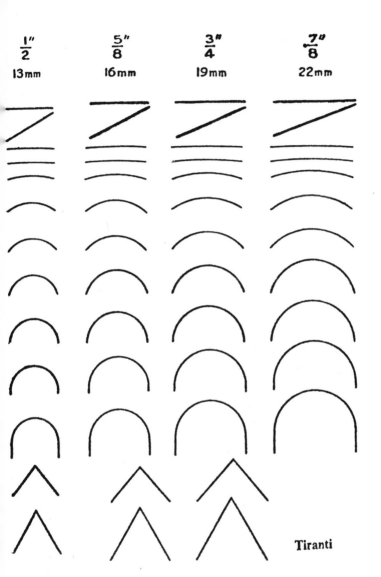

$\frac{1''}{2}$	$\frac{5''}{8}$	$\frac{3''}{4}$	$\frac{7''}{8}$
13mm	16mm	19mm	22mm

Tiranti

17

gouge but deeper, with sides that are parallel or slightly tapering away from each other; the veiner is similar in section but with deeper sides. The V tool is shaped as its name suggests, and is made in three different angles, 45°, 60°, and 90°, of which 60° is the most useful.

Three other shapes of tool are to be found in manufacturers' catalogues: they are the macaroni, the fluteroni, and the backeroni. These have a section like three sides of a rectangle, and were obviously designed for special purpose commercial work. They are not much used today.

In order to maintain a consistent standard of manufacture, woodcarving tools are classified in three ways: shape, that is, whether straight, curved or bent; width at the cutting edge in inches or millimetres; and thirdly, section, referring to the shape at the cutting edge, whether chisel, gouge, or V. A number corresponding to this code is stamped on the shaft.

The series begins at number one, which is a flat chisel; number two is a skew chisel, its cutting edge being at 45° to the shaft; then the gouges start at number three, with the radius of curvature decreasing as the number progresses, up to number nine, which is a true semi-circle; number ten is a fluter, and number eleven the veiner. The chart in fig. 4 shows the most popular shapes and sizes. Few tools are made over one inch in width, beyond which size they are difficult to control.

Some suppliers sell tools without handles, for the benefit of those carvers who prefer to make their own, and it is an advantage if all the handles do not conform to one pattern or size, but vary in shape and weight to suit the tool, so that it is well balanced and comfortable to hold.

Ash is the wood most commonly used for handles, but many others are suitable: mahogany, walnut, boxwood and sycamore, the softer woods being used for the smaller tools which would never be hit with a mallet. An added advantage of having handles of a variety of shapes and colours is that one can quickly identify a particular tool when there are a dozen or more on the bench together.

There are important points to remember when making and fitting a handle: the hole to take the chisel or gouge must be drilled in the centre of the handle, and it must be concentric in order that the shaft of the tool is in a straight line with the handle. If the handle is octagonal or square in section, the cutting edge of the tool must be parallel with one of the flat faces.

To ensure the alignment of tool and handle, it is advisable to drill the hole in the wood before the handle is shaped, then to drive in the tool lightly to test for straightness. Any discrepancy can be corrected by shaping the handle to suit.

The hole should be drilled sufficiently deep to take the tool to within about $\frac{1}{4}''$ of the shoulder. Then, with the tool held firmly in a vice, gently tap the handle with a mallet until it reaches the shoulder. The handle can then be finished with a rasp or spokeshave, and finally sandpapered and polished.

There are a few other woodworking tools that a carver will find useful. Firstly, a handsaw or crosscut saw for removing large sections of wood, a coping saw for cutting out thin sections and pierced relief work, a plane for making good joints, and a spokeshave for shaping convex surfaces on abstract work or the exterior of bowls and dishes.

Rasps and files can be useful for blending together large areas of form, particularly in hard woods where the surfaces are to be sandpapered and polished. They should be used with care on soft woods, as the file marks will penetrate deeply into the wood and may have to be chiselled out.

The modern shaping tools stamped out in sheet steel have sharp, non-clogging teeth. They are obtainable in flat, convex and round sections, and are excellent over large areas and on end grain. 337.754/736.4

Another recent design of file is one that is circular in section, 8″ or 9″ long, with a central core of soft metal which makes it possible to bend the file to the shape required for a particular piece. This is naturally a once only operation.

Rifflers are small files shaped at each end and used for getting into awkward corners that are difficult to reach with a chisel or gouge. They have the same disadvantage as all files in that they leave unsightly scratches on the wood.

Scrapers made from flexible, tempered spring steel between .010″ and .015″ are ideal for the smooth finishing of convex shapes and removing file marks. If properly sharpened, they are cutting tools that take off a fine shaving, leaving a clean surface to the wood.

Although tools can be purchased in what suppliers term as standard, amateur, or professional kits, there always seems to be one or two which never get used. The following tools, which I have chosen as being suitable for a beginner, are those which get the most use for all types of work, and these I would not be without. They can be added to according to the type of work; for large work choose a similar number of tool, but increase the width.

½″ No 1, or a good quality carpenter's chisel
½″ No 4 and No 6 gouges
⅜″ No 5 gouge, ¼″ No 8 gouge
¼″ No 39 parting tool
$3/16$″ No 11 fluter.

When not in use, tools should be protected from damage to the edges, and a most convenient and practical method is the tool roll shown in fig. 5. A piece of material is folded towards the centre and a row of pockets stitched down on each side to fit the handles. The material can be green baize, chamois leather, or even strong canvas, and a length of tape should be stitched at one end so that it can be tied round the middle when rolled.

If tools are not used for a long period, they should be wiped with an oily rag to prevent rust.

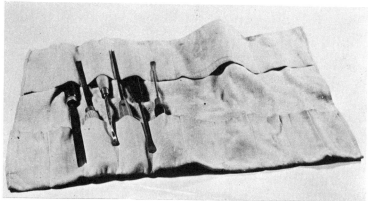

Fig. 5 Tool roll.

Although a certain amount of small work can be done on the kitchen table, a firm, sturdy, although not necessarily large, bench is required for heavy work. Its height should be from 33″ to 39″, length from 36″ upwards, and width 24″. The thickness of the top, which can be constructed of three boards, should be a minimum of 1½″ on the front boards where the majority of work will be fixed.

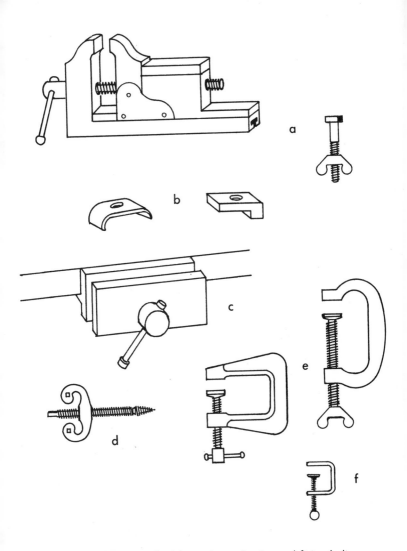

Fig. 6 Methods of fixing work: (a) woodcarver's vice and fixing bolt
(b) wood or metal buttons (c) carpenter's vice (d) bench screw
(e) G cramps (f) thumbscrew.

The most common way of holding work is in a vice. The carver's vice or chops (fig. 6a) is held on top of the bench by a bolt tightened with a wing nut from underneath. This enables it to be rotated, or drawn forward to overhang the bench so as to accommodate large and irregular shaped work. For most purposes, however, the carpenter's vice (fig. 6c), which fits flush with the bench, is quite satisfactory, particularly if the screw has a quick release to enable work to be changed from one position to another.

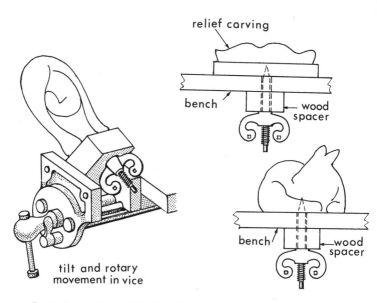

tilt and rotary movement in vice

Fig. 7 Application of the bench screw.

The carver's bench screw (fig. 6d) is suitable for holding low relief panels or work in the round; it also has the advantage of quick release, so that work may be easily rotated. One end has a taper 'V' thread which is screwed into the work, and the main body has a parallel square thread that goes through a hole in the bench, is held by a wing nut and spacing washer, and is used to shorten the length of engagement (fig. 7).

G cramps (clamps) are always useful, particularly those with a deep throat which will reach well in from the edge of the bench (fig. 6e).

The easiest way to hold a panel or low relief is with a metal or wooden clip or button (fig. 6b), screwed into the bench with one end resting on the work.

Whatever method is used for fixing the work, it must be held firm to the bench and not move when being carved.

Mallets should be round, and are obtainable in different weights with beech, lignum vitae or metal heads. They should not be too large or too heavy for comfort, for their purpose is not only to remove as much wood as possible in the shortest time, but to allow greater control over the tool when carving the smaller details in hard wood, or when using the parting tool to follow a carefully drawn outline such as an engraved pattern on a dish, the centre line of a leaf, or incised lettering.

3 Sharpening tools

When everything else fails, read the instructions. (Old Adage)

Unfortunately for the beginner, woodcarving tools cannot nowadays be bought sharpened ready for use, unless they are obtained secondhand from friends or other woodcarvers, which is a good source for them as they will have been well used and tested. But a good tool, well looked after, will last for several generations, so they do not often appear on the secondhand market. Whether purchased new or second-hand, it is important to know how to maintain tools in good condition, how to repair damaged edges and produce the razor-like sharpness necessary for the production of good work. They should be examined and tested at the beginning of every job, and sharpened to perfection for the finishing stages of the carving.

Sharpening stones

The stones used for sharpening need to be fast cutting yet capable of producing a fine edge on the steel. A wood-carver's box of stones will contain a great variety of shapes and textures collected over the years as the number of his tools increase, and they will have names like Charnley Forres, Turkey and Washita, many of which are now rare.

There are, however, at least four useful types of oilstone on the market today. They are carborundum, India, Washita and Arkansas. The first two are manufactured stones, and are made in coarse, medium and fine grades moulded into various shapes. The latter are natural stones and, as their names indicate, are from America; they are necessary for producing the finest cutting edge on the steel. The minimum number of stones to acquire for sharpening the majority of chisels and gouges would be a medium grade carborundum and a Washita, both slipstones. After sharpening on the stone, the tool needs to be stropped to remove any remaining fine particles of steel and to produce the razor-like edge. The strop should be of soft leather and have worked into it a mixture of fine emery powder or crocus powder blended with tallow. The mixture is best applied hot and stropped well in; oil should never be used on a strop.

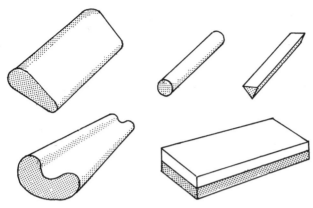

Fig. 8 Types of sharpening stones.

Carving tools differ from other wood-working tools in as much as both sides of the tool are used, and therefore both sides have to be honed. This is why slipstones have convex edges to use for the inside of the gouges. Most tools when purchased have never seen an oilstone and are ground only on the outside. The bevel is usually at the correct angle, which is approximately 15°, a comfortable working angle.

The slipstone holder. See figs. 9 and 10.

This can be made from any available wood. The centre portion, about ⅜" thick, is shaped to a taper exactly that of the slipstone. It should be about 2" longer than the longest stone to be used, and of a width about equal to the stone.

On the flat side, a parallel strip about ¾" wide and ³/₁₆" thick is glued and pinned at one end; at the opposite end, a piece of the same thickness is cut, long enough to reach the end with the slipstone in position. A saw cut is made through this piece, at an angle approximately 10° to 15°, dividing it into two equal parts. One part is fixed to the end of the holder, the other becomes the wedge to hold the stone in position (see fig. 9).

Turn the work over and follow the same procedure on the opposite side, only in this case the wedge is already made and the end pieces must taper in thickness in order to bring them parallel to and level with the stone. Wedges are made of different widths to suit the various lengths of stones. To prevent the holder moving when in use, a piece of thin plywood the width of the distance between the two ends, without the wedge, is tacked to the bench. When fitted to this, the holder will not move during the sharpening process. For the more experienced woodworker, the holder can be made from one piece of wood.

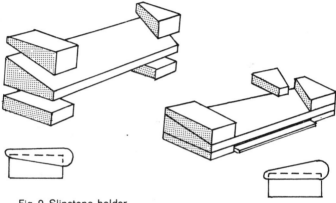

Fig. 9 Slipstone holder.

The chisel

Begin by sharpening the chisel first on the carborundum or India stone to remove the grinding marks. Some manufactured stones are made with a coarse grade on one surface and a finer grade on the reverse, or a slipstone can be used with its face level. The stone should be located firmly on the bench between two fillets of wood tacked on to the bench, or in a holder as show in fig. 9. It is not possible to sharpen the tool if the stone is moving around. Using a light thin lubricating oil to prevent the stone getting clogged, lay the chisel flat on its bevel, holding it in one hand with the forefinger pointing towards the cutting edge. This will give full control over the direction of movement. Then, with the fingers of the other hand resting firmly on the back of the tool, push forwards and backwards the full length of the stone, exerting pressure on the forward stroke. Take care to keep the angle of the tool constant throughout the movement, which should cover the whole area of the stone to avoid wearing a hollow down the centre. (See fig. 10).

Wipe the tool occasionally to check the bevel, and see that it is not being rubbed down more on one side than the other. Test the edge by gently drawing a finger down the back and over the tip, and when you feel the burr or wire edge, turn the tool over and repeat the process to remove the grinding marks from the other side of the chisel, so that there are two carving positions. Now change over to the Washita stone. Lubricate well, keep the tool at the same angle, and continue rubbing first one side and then the other until the burr is worn off. In the finishing stages, less pressure is required, otherwise it will be difficult to remove the burr and you will be continually creating a fresh one. The sharpening is now finished by stropping. Hold the tool down at the front of the strop on the correct bevel angle and, maintaining a firm pressure, draw it sharply backwards away from the cutting edge for about a dozen strokes on each side of the tool.

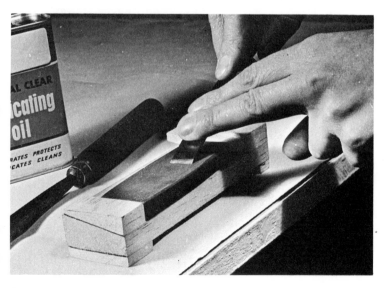

Fig. 10 Sharpening the chisel.

Now is the time to test the tool for sharpness, and the best wood for this is yellow pine or a similar soft wood. A piece of this should always be available for testing the cutting edges, for although a tool may appear to be cutting clean in a hard, strong grained timber, it is only when used on soft pine that gaps in the cutting edge can be detected. Test cuts should always be made across the grain, and should produce a smooth clean surface. To use a carver's expression, the tool should whistle through the wood. There is no wood that cannot be carved by a tool that cuts cleanly across the grain of yellow pine.

The gouge

Having successfully sharpened the chisel, next try the gouge, commencing with the outside or convex side. The angle of a slipstone is approximately equal to the bevel angle of the tool, and if the stone is laid flat on the bench or in a holder as illustrated in figs. 11 and 12, and the gouge laid on it horizontally and at right angles to the length of the stone, it should be resting on its outer bevel. It may have to be raised or lowered slightly to accommodate a shorter or longer bevel.

Instead of rubbing lengthwise as in sharpening a chisel, the movement is across the cutting edge. The gouge is held in one hand, with the thumb on top and the fingers of the other hand exerting pressure on the tool as it moves from left to right and back across the stone. As the gouge moves across to the right, the hand holding it slowly rotates to the left or anti-clockwise, and in moving the gouge back to the left, the hand rotates the tool to the right. In this manner the full face of the bevel is rubbed evenly, but care must be taken not to turn too far at the end of the travel or the corner of the tool will be rounded.

When all the grinding marks have been removed, turn your attention to the inside of the tool. With a new tool, there is no bevel ground on the inside, so it is left to the carver to sharpen to his own taste or requirements. Certainly the tool can be made to cut by just removing the burr after the outside has been honed, but with straight gouges of curves from No. 3 to No. 6 inclusive, which are used equally on the inside and outside, a bevel is required on the inside, although this needs to be only about one third

Figs 11, 12 Sharpening the gouge, outside bevel.

as long as the outside bevel and of course at the same angle.

Choose a coarse or medium grade slipstone with a radius which will fit the inside of the tool. The radius can be slightly smaller, but never larger or flatter, otherwise the corners of the stone will wear grooves and make the edge of the tool uneven. The radius on the edge of a slipstone, when new, is continuous throughout its length and it is advisable, therefore, to modify this by making one end flatter. The stones are easily shaped on a grindstone or with coarse emery paper, and the ends can also be shaped so that one or two stones can be adapted to sharpen a considerable range of gouges.

The method of honing the inside of the gouge is similar to that of sharpening the chisel. There are two ways of doing this: first, by rubbing the tool along the radiused edge of the stone, holding it at the correct angle. It should be moved backwards and forwards in the direction of the shaft, and combined with a slight turning movement to ensure that the whole of the bevel is covered evenly. The alternative method, which is better for larger sizes, is to lay the tool on the edge of the bench and rub the stone across

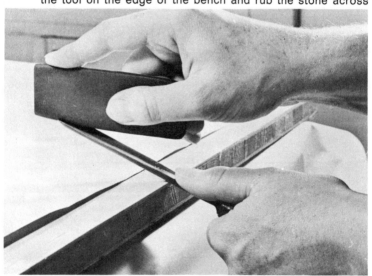

Fig. 13 Sharpening the inside bevel.

the bevel, incorporating a side to side movement with the forward and backward stroke (fig. 13). When a good inside bevel has been achieved, the tool should be finished with the Washita stone both inside and out until the burr is removed. The tool should then be stropped in the same manner as the chisel, that is, lengthwise. The inside radius can be stropped with the leather folded over the edge of the bench or round a piece of shaped wood. When using the strop, all tools must be drawn away from the cutting edge. Never push them forward or sideways, as this action would only result in cutting the strop.

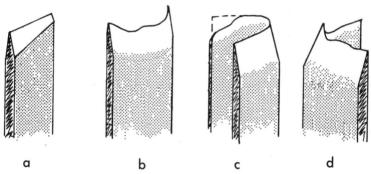

| a | b | c | d |

Fig. 14 Sharpening faults: (a) uneven bevel on chisel (b) wavy cutting edge on gouge (c) corner rubbed off fluter (d) hooked point on parting tool.

Points to remember at this stage: keep the stone well lubricated, otherwise the particles of metal that are being removed will clog the pores. When testing the tool for sharpness, do not hold the wood in one hand and the tool in the other; a slip could cause a nasty cut. If a tool should roll off the bench or drop from your hand, do not attempt to catch it. It is far better to have a blunt tool than a hole in your hand. At all times, both in sharpening and carving, both hands should remain behind the cutting edge.

The fluter or veiner

This is sharpened in a similar way to the gouge. The inside needs very little chamfer, but it should be rubbed down

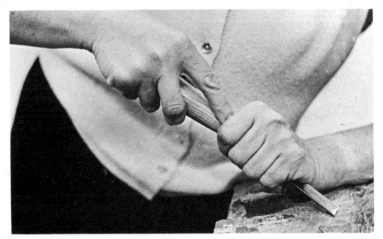

Fig. 15 Correct method of holding tool for carving.

evenly each side as well as at the bottom radius. The slip-stone should be narrow enough to rub each side independently, and not be a tight fit inside the tool.

The outside chamfer on gouges, although described as a 15° bevel, does not have to be absolutely accurate or mechanically flat. It is an advantage to have a slight radius where the bevel meets the shaft to remove what is known as the heel.

The parting tool

This useful tool is probably the most difficult to sharpen. Although the two sides can be treated as flat chisels, it is at the point where they meet that the most attention is required. No attempt should be made to try and keep it a sharp point; it should be treated as a small radius blending into the flat at each side. Sharpened in this manner, its cut is more effective and the tool is easier to control.

Start as before on the outer bevel, treating each side as a chisel and making the bevel equal on each outer face. This will result in a sharp corner where the two planes meet. Now consider this point as a gouge: lay the tool on its left hand bevel, at right angles to the stone as in sharpening a gouge; draw it slowly across the stone to the left, at the

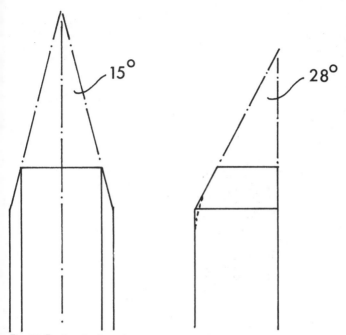

Fig. 16 Parting tool angles.

same time rotating the tool to the right and finishing the stroke at the left-hand end of the stone, flat on the bevel of the other face. Stop the rotating movement as soon as the flat face contacts the stone. This stroke is then repeated in reverse, and continued backwards and forwards across the stone until a small radius is formed at the tip. There is an important point that needs consideration when forming a radius at the angle of a parting tool, as reference to fig. 16 will show. It will be observed that if the angle of bevel of a 60° parting tool No. 41 is 15° to an axis parallel to the shaft of the tool, then at the point where these two planes meet, the angle produced is a little over 28° to the same axis. This has the effect of forming a hump or heel on the back of the tool, producing a different cutting angle at the corner than on the sides, which will restrict the free cutting of the tool and cause it to stutter when carving a

33

sapele

Douglas fir

sweet chestnut

African walnut

birch

jarrah

Afrormosia

European beech

American red oak

green heart

sycamore

European elm

jelutong

central American mahogany

ash

Burma teak

radius. This heel must therefore be rounded to blend not only with the side bevels but also with the back edge of the tool.

The inside of the parting tool should be honed with the triangular section of the Arkansas stone, making sure that the sharp edge of the stone has been rounded on a grindstone or with emery paper to a radius suitable for the point where the two flats meet. The inside bevel need only be small - little more than necessary to remove the burr - but it should be even, the corner radius blending smoothly into the sides, which must be kept straight.

If the cutting edge of a tool becomes irregular, due to using an incorrect radius slipstone or by rubbing down more on one side than another, the tool should be held at right-angles to the stone and rubbed down until the edge is straight and square with the shaft. It can then be re-sharpened.

Fig. 18 Tropical fish. Willow.

4 Carving in relief

Relief carving can be described as two-dimensional in as much as it is designed to be viewed normally from one position only. As the effect of colour and form is achieved by cutting into the wood at varying depths and at different angles, to reflect or subdue the light according to the function of the design, it follows that the majority of relief carvings are designed to suit the particular lighting in which they are to be placed.

When relief carving is applied to furniture, a further point has to be taken into account and is the main consideration for this type of work: that it can be freely handled and has no sharp corners or rough edges that can do damage to clothes or persons.

There are three main types of relief carving. Firstly, where the complete work is carved from one piece of wood or, with large works, from several pieces glued together. Here the outline of the design is drawn on the wood, and the spaces between and around the design carved away to a predetermined depth as a background.

Secondly, where the outline of the design is cut out by bandsaw or, if by hand, with a coping saw or fretsaw, and is glued on to a background of a similar or contrasting wood.

Thirdly, where the work is designed to be seen in outline or silhouette and is cut out as before with a saw. It is usually free standing, without a background, and is viewed from either or both sides, as in church screens.

The most satisfactory lighting for viewing or carving a relief is either from the top or from the left, or from any point between the two. A direct front light will tend to flatten all the modelling and subdue the detail. As most relief carving is done on a bench, the effect of top lighting is obtained if the bench is situated in front of a window.

Carving an oak leaf ·

For the first exercise in carving a relief I have chosen the oak leaf, because its outline is particularly suitable for drawing with the tool shapes.

Pick yourself an oak leaf; it should keep fresh enough for you to finish the exercise. Lay it on a flat surface and note the contours and at which points the leaf touches the

Fig. 19 Natural oak leaf.

ground. Make a full size drawing in order to learn the main characteristics of the leaf, then lay the leaf on your drawing to check which points you have missed. Having corrected your outline, trace this on to the wood. Measure on the leaf the highest point from the ground and make a pencil line at this distance round the edge of the wood to indicate the level of the ground.

With the fluter, carve a groove all round the outline of the leaf about ⅛″ from the line (fig. 20), then using a ½″

Fig. 20 Removing the background.

No. 9 or similar gouge start cutting from the front edge of the wood across the grain and up to the outline groove. Continue along the full length of the wood and down to the pencil line. Repeat on the opposite side of the leaf, and while you have this tool in your hand use it to set down the outline a little closer to the line (fig. 21).

Fig. 21 Setting down.

Having cleared away the surrounding waste wood, now choose tools which more closely fit the outline - the fluter and a No. 4 gouge from ⅜″ to ½″ wide should be suitable - and set down on the line all round the shape of the leaf. No undercutting should be done at this stage, and the shape should be vertical as though it had been cut with a fretsaw. Level off the ground with a flat or slightly hollow tool and the work is ready for shaping.

Fig. 22 First stage.

With the No. 9 gouge carve the main hollows through the leaf, dividing it up into its individual forms; observe how they all flow from the centre line. Continue modelling with the No. 4 gouge, linking the shapes together and using the inside of the tool for the tips of the serrations where the forms are convex; then take the hollows right down to the background where those parts of the leaf touch the ground. Do not try to smooth the surface, but take smaller cuts to blend in the softer shapes.

Fig. 23 Second stage.

Fig. 24 Finished carving.

When surface modelling is finished, and not before, set down the outline to the final shape and undercut only where the edges are thick. Do not leave a knife-like edge anywhere, but always finish a sharp edge with a slight chamfer; this will accentuate the drawing with a highlight.

The background can now be finished, working right to the outline of the leaf, where a smaller tool may be necessary to reach into the narrow corners. As a general principle, it is advisable always to use the largest tool possible for working; it will help to keep the character and simplicity of the design. The use of too many small tools is a temptation to add unnecessary and fussy detail in which the main character of the design gets lost.

A refinement would be to add the centre line, using a parting tool, with either a single line or, as in the example, a tapering vein. This will need a little care; the line should first be drawn on the wood with pencil, and here you may discover the impossibility of drawing a good flowing line on an irregular surface. This must first be corrected, then practised on a piece of waste wood.

When carving a groove with a parting tool, keep the tool resting in the groove. Cut the line with a series of short cuts, drawing the tool back into the groove after each cut.

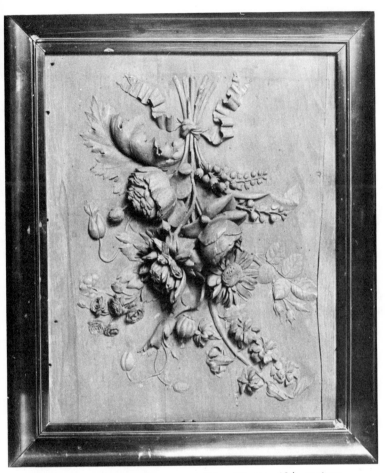

Fig. 25 Spray of flowers. Pear wood, 38 x 32 cm., 19th century.
(Reitlinger Bequest, Maidenhead, Berks, England.)

Complete control over the tool is only obtainable if the forearm or wrist is resting firmly on the bench or work.

The tools used in carving this example were ¼″ No. 11, ½″ No. 9, ⁷/₁₆″ No. 4, the parting tool ¼″ No. 39 for the stem and a ½″ No. 3 for the background.

Fig. 26 Cypher of Sir Henry Puckering, by Grinling Gibbons. (Trinity College, Cambridge. Crown copyright.)

Having completed the exercise, try other types of leaf; there is an infinite variety. Then use a group of two or three. Cut a spray from a tree or bush, noting the arrangement and method of growth. Flowers can also be attempted. A fine example of naturalistic carving can be seen in fig. 25; this of course is a technical exercise and not suitable for architectural design. A successful use of natural forms is seen in the well balanced design containing the cypher of Sir Henry Puckering (fig. 26), a panel about 21″ by 15″ now in the library of Trinity College, Cambridge, and executed by that master of English woodcarvers, Grinling Gibbons.

Carved relief applied to background

The subject I have selected as an exercise in the second method of carving a relief is a little swallow (fig. 27). Although simple in outline, it is full of the movement characteristic of the bird in flight, with open mouth feeding on

Fig. 27 Completed carving of swallow.

flies and insects as it darts swiftly through the air. The model illustrated is about 4 inches across and about ⅝ of an inch thick. It should be measured and drawn carefully at full size on paper first, in order to get the correct lines and proportions, for once the outline has been cut in wood there is no changing it (fig. 28). Choose a firm textured but not too hard wood, lime, mahogany, pear or similar. The material can be stained if desired when finished to suit a particular colour combination. Trace the outline on the wood, with the direction of grain running from head to tail. The direction of grain is a very important factor when designing for wood. The main consideration is strength, for

Fig. 28 Full size outline drawing of swallow.

if in the case of the swallow the grain ran across the body of the bird, not only would it be more difficult to carve, for all the cutting of the wings should be across the grain, but the tips of the feathers and the beak would easily snap off and the base of the tail at the narrowest point would break off from the body of the bird.

Another point to reckon with is the pattern and arrangement of the grain markings. These can sometimes be selected to emphasise a particular area or form, but in the case of the swallow this is not important. The wood chosen should be even grained not strongly marked, for in this design the basic characteristics of the design are line and not form.

With a small subject like this, it is better to carve more than one at a time; any mistake or accident can be corrected on the second or third, and it is surprising how much quicker and with how much more confidence a repetition is carved.

Fig. 29 (a) First stage, isolating individual forms (b) setting the angle of tail and wings (c) subdividing the wings into main groups of feathers (d) outlining the feathers and undercutting.

Having cut round close to the outline with a padsaw, fretsaw or other means, the work should be glued to a piece of background wood. Sandwiched between the work and the background should be a sheet of newsprint or similar texture paper; this will prevent the glue from holding too fast, and facilitates the lifting of the work from the background when finished.

When the glue has set, fix the board to the bench with any of the fixtures described in chapter 2.

With a deep gouge divide the work up into the principal masses (fig. 29a). Then, with a flatter gouge and beginning with the wings and tail, shape each individual mass at its correct angle and form in relation to the body of the bird (fig. 29b). Set the head at the correct angle, then subdivide each wing into its two main groups of feathers (fig. 29c). Finish shaping the body and head, with occasional reference to the end profile; a gouge cut will suggest the open beak - do not attempt to drill a hole there - then carefully draw in pencil on the wings the individual feathers before carving their outline with the parting tool. Now with a small slightly hollow gouge, sink one side of each feather so that it appears to lie under the one next to it (fig. 29d). It is important to sink at the correct edge, for it doesn't matter what type of bird you are depicting as all wing structures are anatomically identical. So check the arrangement with the next bird you happen to see.

When you are satisfied with the surface modelling, start to undercut the wings and tail feathers and shape round the head (fig. 30e). Reduce thick edges and undercut as much as possible before lifting off the background; it should come away easily. Using a flat chisel inserted at the paper level, tap gently from the thickest parts of the work. It can

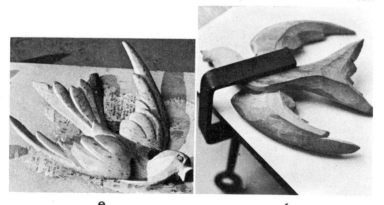

e   f
Fig. 30 (e) Undercutting (f) chamfering the back.

Fig. 31 Stall end. Oak. Dutch, 16th century. (Victoria and Albert Museum. Crown copyright.)

then be turned over, held down with a small thumbscrew and the back chamfered off (fig. 30f). After trimming the tips of the feathers, a small rasp or sandpaper will remove the rough edges.

The work can now be stained and polished or even painted in natural colours, and will look well mounted on a square or circular background.

Carving an outline

The third type of relief carving is that which is viewed from both sides. Each side should be a complete and satisfying design in itself, although in figure work which has to tell a story, one side is usually more important, as in the church stall end shown in fig. 31.

Figs. 32, 33, 36, are simple examples of this style, whose main attractions are flowing lines, colour, and grain pattern.

Form and modelling are not the most important considerations, except where they are used to vary the pattern of the grain markings. These three subjects demonstrate the unique qualities of wood as a sculptural medium; none of these works could be reproduced in any other material and be so effective. In plaster, plastic, or bronze they would look dead, not only in appearance but to the touch; they would have lost the good to handle feel of wood. They are individual works which cannot be reproduced, even in another piece of wood, for it would never have exactly the same grain markings and colour.

Fig. 32 Horse head, low relief profile. Pine.

5 Chip and surface carving

In practically all known civilisations and in all periods of history there are to be found examples of the art or craft of chip carving. Used by the Egyptians for decorating household equipment, furniture and burial caskets, skilfully developed in Scandinavian countries and as far north as Iceland, it has been applied to spinning wheel heads, mangle boards, bible boxes, butter moulds and barn doors. A similarity of design and pattern can be traced in carvings from places and periods of time so remote that these ideas could not possibly have been passed on. The presumption is that the basic shapes were decided by the tools that were available, and these appear to have been a knife or chisel, and a gouge. There is an exception to this similarity in the work of the Maori natives of New Zealand, whose wave-like scrolls and scalloped designs do not appear in the Northern hemisphere, may be because they had no metal tools but used the sharp edges of stones and sea shells. However, it is the chisel and gouge that we use today.

The chisel is used to produce the triangular pocket and the gouge for the notch or thumbnail cut. These two patterns form the basis from which all incised carving has evolved, and are two cuts with a common meeting point.

One cut is set in square with the surface of the wood, the second at an angle to meet it, and a chip is thereby removed. That is the principle; in practice, it can take more than one cut and more than one chip, according to the size and shape of the notch or pocket.

The basic cuts are illustrated on pages 54 and 56, and to achieve proficiency in cutting these is time well spent in the use and control of the carving tool. Start with the vertical cuts, using a ½ inch or ⅜ inch chisel. Choose a moderately soft wood with no strong grain marking - yellow pine, jelutong or Honduras mahogany. With the surface planed smooth and flat, draw parallel lines the width of the tool apart and the full length of the wood, in the direction of the grain. Divide this length into squares by eye, or by using the tool width as a guide.

Hold the chisel square with the wood and on the vertical line and press in as deep as the wood will allow. The tool should be held in the same manner as for setting in (fig. 21),

Fig. 33 Horse heads. Rosewood.

Fig. 34 Bowl. English walnut.

Fig. 35 Oak chest. Scottish, 16th century. (Victoria and Albert Museum. Crown copyright.)

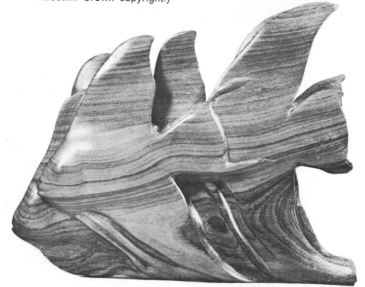

Fig. 36 Angel fish. Rosewood.

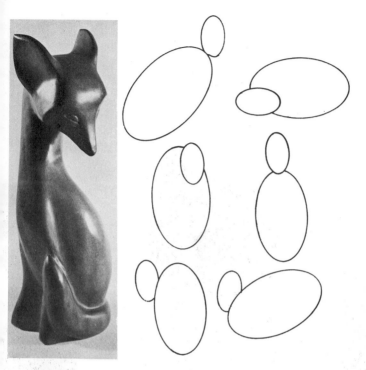

Fig. 51 Fox. Mahogany.   Fig. 52 Arrangements of egg shapes.

front of another, so if photographs are used obtain as many as possible, and if taking them yourself, get at least one plan view as well as elevations from all directions, for these are to be working drawings or illustrations.

Having thoroughly familiarised yourself with the subject to the extent of being able to make sketches from memory, make a three-dimensional model in wax or plasticine. This is preferable to clay, as it will not shrink in size or crack. It should be of a definite proportion to the finished work, 1/4, 1/3 or 1/2 full size, and like the sketches it is not intended to be an exhibition work. But it is necessary to get all the proportions and forms in correct relation to each other; the masses must be accurately positioned, as this is the final three-dimensional working model.

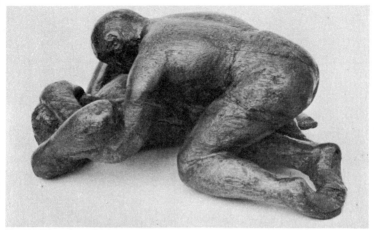

Fig. 54 Wrestlers. Mahogany.

Very few sculptors would consider working without a sketch model, however small, for it is here that the final composition is decided. Before the first chip is removed, with the aid of these preliminary exercises he has in his mind a complete vision of the finished work, in contrast to those artists with a Micawber-like attitude who go chipping away in the hope that something will turn up.

As these sketch models are only a means to an end, and are rarely retained once the work is completed, there are very few examples remaining. The Victoria and Albert Museum in London have one or two by Italian sculptors. Illustrated in fig. 55 is one by Michelangelo, a sketch model for a life-size figure in marble, one of a group of slaves. There is no fussy detail here, but all the main forms are correctly related. Note how the pose is designed to fit a block of marble; it would be equally suitable for wood, with no arms or legs waving in the air without support and liable to be easily damaged.

I think it was Michelangelo who was once asked to criticise a composition by another sculptor. After studying it carefully, he suggested that it should be rolled down a hill, and that what remained would be a considerable improvement.

Fig. 53 Pelican. English oak. Vulture. Lime wood and stained walnut. Toucan. Ebony. Cat. Mahogany. Tropical fish. Willow. Leaf dish. Mahogany.

Fig. 55 Sketch model of a slave by Michelangelo. (Victoria and Albert Museum. Crown copyright.)
Fig. 56 Preliminary stage of carving in oak, working from sketch model.

A single figure is well designed if it will fit into a niche, and if like other great thinkers you enjoy contemplating the problems and complexities of modern life whilst relaxing in the bath, you will discover that any pose that is possible within the confines of your surroundings is quite practical for executing in wood.

Having decided upon your subject and completed your studies as far as making a sketch model in plasticine, next prepare the wood. Carefully measure the height, width and thickness of your model, and multiply these figures to the desired magnification to obtain the size of wood required. Add an inch or more on the height to allow for a base to be used for holding the work down to the bench or in a vice; if this is square or rectangular, it can also be used as a datum for measuring from.

As a subject for demonstration I have chosen a familiar domestic animal, the cat. The wood is seven inches high, six inches wide, and five inches thick, and is Honduras mahogany. Owing to the difficulty of obtaining well seasoned wood of this thickness, it was built from two-and-a-half-inch thick wood with a joint down the centre. Make a full size profile drawing and trace it on opposite sides of the wood. A sawcut is made into the deepest point and also around the base, about a half inch deep on all four sides in order that the squareness is maintained. The profile is then cut through across the wood, with a ½″ to ¾″ gouge, No. 6 or 7. With this tool and a 5/16″ or ⅜″ fluter, most of the roughing out work can be done (fig. 57a). Referring to the

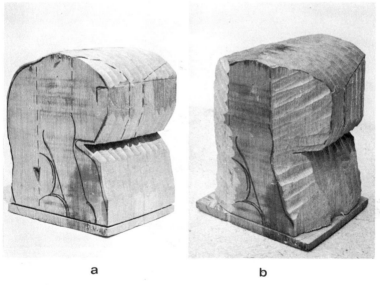

a   b

Fig. 57 (a) Profile drawn on wood and shaped (b) corners chamfered.

73

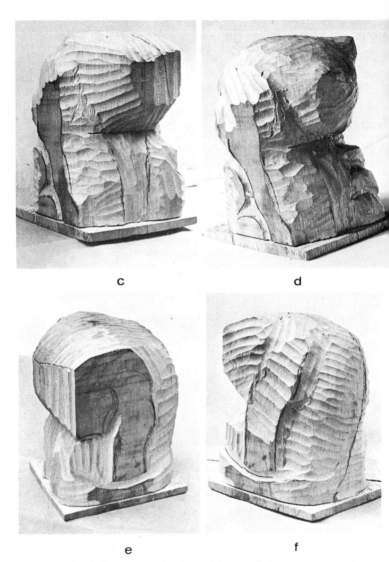

c   d

e   f

Fig. 58 (c, d) Separating the forms (e) stage b from opposite side
(f) main forms indicated.

74

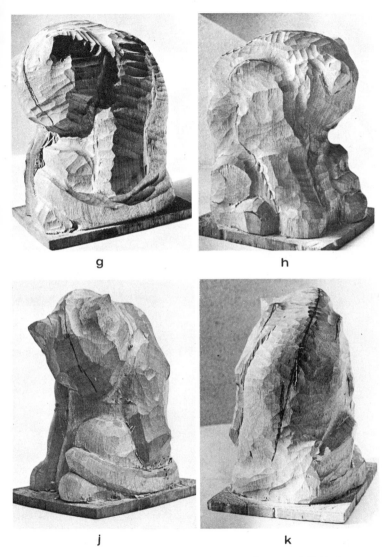

Fig. 59 (g) Main forms indicated (h, j) main forms subdivided (k) back view.

| l | m |

Fig. 60 (l) Blending details together (m) chisel cut finish.

model, mark off on the wood the angle of the head relative to the body and a chamfer down the back; cut away the wood, working close to the line and keeping the planes simple with no attempt at rounding (fig. 57e).

The next step is to sub-divide the general shape into separate masses, the head, front legs, rear legs, and tail. Draw around these with a fluter, and then working on one item at a time, bring them all one stage further, commencing with the head. The most prominent points should always be positioned first: in this case it is the tips of the ears, and these must be very accurately positioned as they also determine the angle of the head. Measure these points carefully from the model, and always keep the construction lines drawn on the wood. Having set the angle of the head, cut it down to size across the width. Draw on the wood a centre line, starting from the tip of the nose, over the back and down to the tail (fig. 58g, k), and using this as a guide shape the convex form from the skull right down the back, ignoring the legs. Concentrate on getting this one form correctly positioned.

Now mark on the wood the position of the shoulder blades, and starting from these points work down the legs, gradually bringing them closer to the body (fig. 59f). Work across the grain as much as possible to avoid tearing the wood, and try to carve as if at each stage in its progress it could be regarded as a finished work. Now working round the base, cut back the feet and tail to their correct positions according to the model, starting from the outside (fig. 59g). Now return again to the head and put in the planes in more detail. Keep the ears prominent and solid; indicate the position of the high cheek bones and narrow down the width of the nose and accurately measure the position of the tip from the base (fig. 59j). Flatter gouges will be useful now at this stage, a half inch No. 4, and three quarter or seven eights No. 3.

The principal forms are now subdivided into the smaller shapes, indicating with flat planes the movement from one form to another. See fig. 59g, h, j, three views from the same position showing the development of planes.

Most single figure subjects have one feature which is the basis of the composition, the structure to which all other forms are complimentary or dependant upon. In the case of the cat, I think it would be the right fore leg, which is taking the weight of the body; it should be firm and strong while the left fore leg, in contrast, is hanging limp.

After each stage of progression, the dimensions and proportions should be checked and construction lines drawn on again. Details like eyes and toes should not be carved until the work is almost completed. A student who attempts to model or carve a head for the first time will usually start with a preconceived idea that the head consists of eyes, nose, and mouth, and will try to carve these details directly into the wood, as a painter might set them down on canvas. Experience will show that a considerable amount of work must be done to produce the basic shape of the head before such detail can be added, and if the bone structure and forms around the eyes and mouth are set in their correct relationship, then no difficulty will be experienced in completing these details. In the case of the cat, these are drawn on the finished form with pencil or crayon, to check the correct position, and then carved with the parting tool and a small gouge, used on the inside to produce a convex form.

Fig. 61 Smooth finish.

As the work nears completion, the tool cuts get smaller, so that the forms flow smoothly into each other. The actual surface finish is left to the artist to decide and will depend on the type of wood used and the position or application of the finished work. With the cat, it seemed that the smooth finish was more desirable; it invited handling, and was a pleasure to touch as well as to view. The surface was smoothed first with a riffler, then with medium and fine sandpaper, using a piece of cork or expanded polystyrene as a rubber. It should be cut to the required shape and the sandpaper folded round it, so that you can get into the small radii. All file marks and scratches should be removed.

The work should be left exposed to the air for several days, when it will darken naturally to a richer colour, or it can be stained with a pale wash of spirit colour and rubbed down again when dry as this will raise the grain. Finally, give it a light polish with polyurethane glaze or shellac varnish. This particular work had a light coat of French polish rubbed down with very fine sandpaper when quite hard to a soft matt finish. Beeswax polish can always be used on top of this, should a more brilliant polish be required.

Making a joint

Although large works are often carved from whole tree trunks, this is not always possible or even desirable. It takes many years for wood to season thoroughly, and if this is not complete, splits and shakes will always occur during the carving.

Well seasoned planks of wood are rarely more than three inches thick, and for work of greater thickness joints must be made.

Until about the middle of the seventeenth century, when adhesives began to be used, all woodwork was dry-jointed and often fixed with wooden pegs; but with present-day glues, it is possible to make joints that are stronger than the wood itself.

Wood to be joined should be matched for colour and direction of grain. The two surfaces should be absolutely flat and tested with a straight-edge, and glue should not be used as a filler but as a key between the surfaces in contact.

Scotch glue or animal glues are satisfactory if used hot, and the two faces of the wood should be warmed to avoid chilling the glue when applied. Cramps should be previously prepared and the work then clamped tightly to force out surplus glue; the edges should be wiped clean with a damp rag and left overnight to set hard.

Much easier to manage are the synthetic resin and casein glues, which are used cold. Cramps are necessary to hold the work in position until dry, and manufacturers' instructions should be adhered to when mixing. Very good and useful too are the glues with an acetate base. These are usually sold in tubes, and are quick drying and convenient for repairing accidental breaks, which should be mended as soon as they occur, before the fibres of the wood become damaged.

Fig. 62 Horse. Rosewood. Malayan, modern. One of a group of eight; design based on an old Chinese legend.

8 Texture and finish

The finished surface texture of a carving usually depends upon its use. For furniture, tableware, and other work that is to be handled, it is important that the surfaces should be smooth and free from rough edges or sharp corners.

These will need a surface treatment, and should be well rubbed down with sandpaper, commencing with the coarser grades. Generally, the harder the wood, the coarser the paper has to be. When all irregularities have been removed, the finer grades are used until all the scratches caused by the stronger papers have disappeared. Always work along the grain if possible. To save wear and tear on the fingers, rubbers can be made from cork, or pieces of expanded polystyrene, shaped to fit the work and wrapped round with the paper. Garnet papers, which are coloured red, usually last longer and cut more quickly than do sand or glass papers. Before sandpaper was invented, which was in the early nineteenth century, sharkskin was commonly used for smoothing woodcarving.

Fig. 63 Horse as Fig. 62.

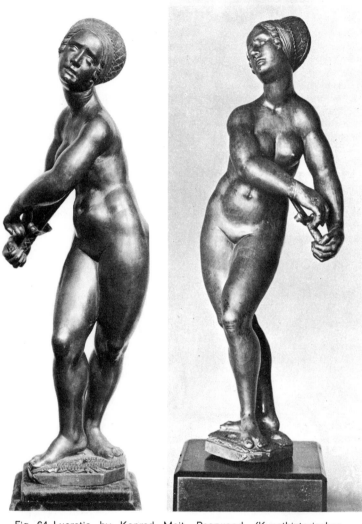

Fig. 64 Lucretia by Konrad Meit. Pearwood. (Kunsthistorisches Museum, Vienna.)

Carving that is not intended for handling, such as architectural and figure work, is best left with the tool cuts showing. It is the shapes, lines and contours of this work that are more important than grain markings, and no amount of sandpapering will improve its appearance. Not only will the labour be wasted, but the work will lose the colour and sparkle caused by the light being reflected from each of the facets and planes of the tool cuts.

With figure carving, particularly large work and life-size portraits, surface texture is important. It is easy to assume that because flesh surfaces are soft and smooth, the wood must be sandpapered thoroughly until it is smooth to the touch. In fact it should be finished to appear smooth to the eye, which is dependent on light reflected from the surface. The smoother the wood is finished, the brighter become the highlights, and a bright highlight indicates a hard surface. However, if the highlight is broken up by small

Fig. 65 Faun. Oak.

regular gouge cuts and still retains the correct contours, then the surface of the work will appear to be much softer.

Similarly, when carving animals or birds, there is the question of how to obtain the effect of fur, hair, or feathers. The treatment should be determined by the scale of the work and the design, whether naturalistic or conventional. The carved bears of Switzerland are usually covered with S-shaped parting tool cuts, a variation of the treatment seen in fig. 41, where the cuts are C-shaped and in rows, giving an heraldic effect and a contrasting colour to the plain background.

In cases where the subject matter is plain and smooth, it is the background which is broken up with tool cuts, and in much of the cheaper quality nineteen-century furniture carving, a metal punch or 'frosting tool' was used to stamp a pattern on the background of carved panels. It was a quick way of clearing the ground of irregularities, but it has a mechanical appearance and destroys the nature and quality of the wood.

The treatment for feathered birds can vary considerably, according to the simplicity of the design and the skill of the carver. In the Gothic periods, the feathers were strongly defined and conventionally grouped in order to be recognised at considerable distances. In the period of Grinling Gibbons and the eighteenth century, the work became more delicate and naturalistic, for it was seen at much closer quarters in the drawing rooms of the country mansions being built and decorated at that time.

There are, of course, no set rules laid down as to how work should be finished, and as the beginner becomes more proficient in the use and control of the tools and material, together with experience and experiment, he will develop naturally an individual style.

Finishing and polishing

Most woods are improved in appearance by a polish that will bring out the natural beauty of the grain and markings; even if the wood is plain, some treatment is necessary to prevent dirt, grease, and moisture from discolouring the work.

Sometimes a change of colour can be an improvement to plain and light coloured woods. Wood stains can be obtained in crystal or powder form which mixes readily with

Fig. 66 Angel with guitar. Limewood. North Rhine, Germany. Carved in 1500, but with very little change of clothing could easily be 20th century. (© Berlin State Museum)

Fig. 67 Chessmen from a set carved in English oak and ebony. Based on 12th-century set in walrus ivory, now in the British Museum. 9 cm high.

methylated spirit, and the various colours can be blended together to produce the desired shade. They should be diluted to a very light tone, and the desired colour arrived at by several applications, allowing each coat to dry before applying the next. Always experiment first on a sample piece of wood, for once the colour is on, it cannot be made lighter. It should be flooded on rapidly and evenly with a soft brush to avoid patches. All colouring should be done before polish is applied.

Wax polish is an excellent finish for hard woods. Beeswax is most commonly used, but Carnuba wax, a product from the palm trees of Brazil, is harder but equally good. The wax should be cut into shavings, put into a flat tin, covered with turpentine and warmed on a hotplate until the wax has melted. When cool, it should be of the consistency of soft butter, and can be applied with a clean rag or an old shaving brush, with a bristle toothbrush to get into corners. Surplus wax should be wiped off, and the work left for a day or two to harden before finally polishing with a soft rag.

With the softer woods and those with a coarse grain, it is an advantage first to give them a very thin coat of French polish or shellac. For lighter woods, use white polish, thinned with spirit; this will raise the grain slightly, and should a smooth finish be required, rub down lightly with fine sandpaper. This treatment will fill the grain, keep the work clean, and is a good base for applying a wax finish. French polish cannot be applied once the wood has been waxed.

Opposite:
Fig. 68 (a) Ruth and Naomi. English walnut (b) Rima. Mahogany (c) Cricketer. Willow (d) Popular Song. Pine.

86

Fig. 69 Family group. Sycamore.

Fig. 70 Virgin and Child, with two angels. South German, 16th century. (Victoria and Albert Museum.)

For work that is handled and tableware, the modern polyurethane glazes are excellent. They are colourless, odourless when dry, and if a brilliant gloss is not required, they can be matted down with glasspaper.

Oil varnishes and varnish stains are not suitable for carved work: they are slow drying, clog up detail, and are inclined to look sticky. Cellulose lacquer, whether brushed or sprayed on, does not wear well and has an unnatural glassy appearance.

When the work is completed, you may feel that a base is desirable. It should not be obtrusive, to draw attention from the work, but be part of the design although not necessarily of the same material. Various shapes and proportions should be tried and modified until the design is satisfactory.

9 Lettering

It could be said that drawing and carving preceded lettering as a means of communication. From scratchings on cave walls to Egyptian hieroglyphics, drawn symbols gradually developed as letters into the Roman Script, the basis of lettering as we know it today.

The main purpose of lettering is to make a statement, deliver a message or order, sometimes gay, light-hearted or sentimental, a noble discourse, secular or sacred; and although the style of letter can be either bold, light, free flowing or decorated, and vary according to the purpose of the inscription, the message should be always clear and legible, and each individual letter easily recognisable.

To satisfy these demands, the following points need careful consideration: the length of the inscription and its position, the area to be occupied, the size of letter to be used and the style, which must be readable from the normal viewing position.

There has been no style in English speaking or European languages to equal that based upon the Roman alphabet (fig. 72). The letters around the base of the Trajan column in Rome are used as a classic example. They are well proportioned and architecturally bold, yet with their varying line thickness and serifs, they maintain a graceful and delicate design. They are suitable for any degree of magnification, but for carving in wood, anything below an inch in height is unsuitable. The grain of the wood is too coarse for delicate drawing. The letters on the Trajan column are about six inches high.

Although of good design, Roman letters should not be used indiscriminately, particularly if the inscription is horizontal with long lengths of line. The Romans used only capital letters, but over a period of many centuries, and with improved methods and materials of writing, there gradually developed the small, or to use a printer's definition the 'lower case', letter. The more accurate although less used definition is the French majuscules for capitals and minuscules for the smaller letters. For long lines of inscription the lower case letter is more suitable; the eye seems to flow more readily along the lines and is not continually halted by verticals; also, more words can be carved in a

Fig. 71 Life-size portrait head. Cedar.

Fig. 72 Roman alphabet.

single line with an equal degree of legibility than with capitals. The two forms of letter can be used in the same inscription, the capitals serving as an emphasis to important words or phrases.

Spacing

This is something about which we can lay down no hard and fast rules. You could measure and make equal the distance between each letter, but the eye does not measure this way; it is continually scanning, following round each letter and up and down the verticals, and what becomes more important is the shape between two letters, rather than the distance between them. The spacing would appear more satisfying to the eye if you were to put an equal area between the letters instead of an equal linear distance.

Adopting this principle as a rough guide to the layout, the smallest distance between two letters would be in a case where two diagonals come together, as in RY or AWAY; it could almost be an overlap. The next would be when two convex shapes come together, as in DO, and then a little larger with one vertical and one convex, as in DI, the greatest distance between any two letters being when two verticals come together.

Just as important is the spacing of the words, and similar rules can apply. They must not be too close to be confusing, or so wide apart that the message does not flow easily. The distance apart of words need not be the same throughout the whole inscription; there may be more letters in one line than another, but the spacing between words in each individual line should be equal, with a minimum of half a letter height between each word.

The spacing of the lines apart is dependent on several conditions, the length of the line, the size of the letters and the general layout. Long lines of words should not be too close together; they become too confusing to follow.

The general design or layout of an inscription is as important as the message it conveys, and many sketches should be made in order to arrive at the most satisfactory arrangement. It may be that a circular or elliptical panel is more pleasing than a rectangle or square, with the more important lines or names in capitals and the general text in lower case, or with large capitals and smaller capitals

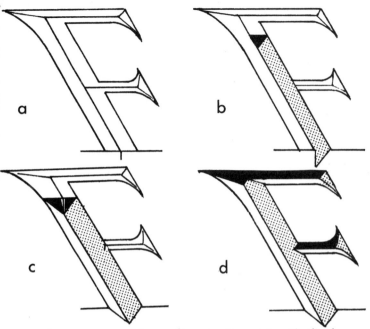

Fig. 73 Cutting an incised letter: (a) centre line set in with chisel (b) right-hand side cut (c) left-hand side, cut to meet at centre (d) horizontals and serifs finished.

as a means of contrast. It is, however, not recommended to use too many different sizes of letter on the same layout. Three should be the maximum, and the difference between the sizes should be sufficiently noticeable, with one size remaining predominant; otherwise, the design of the inscription will become unbalanced.

Punctuation marks as such are rarely used, although it is sometimes necessary with long inscriptions composed of capitals to break these into groups or sentences with a small incised cross, scroll or diamond, which will maintain the overall pattern of letters and yet increase the legibility of the phrase. It is sometimes just sufficient to leave a larger spacing.

A designer may be uncertain when setting out an inscription as to which strokes of a letter should be thick and which thin. Presuming that you are right-handed and write a line of words with a broad pointed pen, you will find that the down strokes or descenders are thick and the upward strokes, or ascenders, are thin. This is the general rule to be followed when laying out lettering. You will notice that with circular shapes like O, the thickest part of the stroke is not exactly on the horizontal centre line but slightly below on the down stroke and above on the upward stroke; this is common to all types of letters based on Roman or Italic.

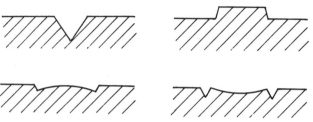

Fig. 74 Sections of carved letters.

The serifs or terminal points of a letter can considerably influence the design of an inscription and are often determined by the material and method of carving. They can be very delicate when incised in close-grained hard wood, and more stumpy in coarser grained material and when they are to be painted and gilded afterwards. The shortest serifs are used on those letters which are raised, as they can be easily damaged.

There are two methods of carving inscriptions in wood. The most effective, from the design and practical point of view, is when letters are incised into the material; they are easier to cut, more readily cleaned and less liable to damage. The section of the letter is approximately a 60° triangle, with the deepest point on the centre line. The second method is to draw the letters on the wood and remove all the surrounding wood to a depth relative to the size of letter, so that the inscription appears to be applied to a background. This method takes considerably longer and is suitable only for short inscriptions.

After having made several sketches to determine the best arrangement of the inscription, it should be drawn full size. This is best done with a chisel-shaped lead pencil, the letters first being sketched in lightly until final positions are decided.

The panel should be prepared with the grain of the wood running horizontally, and the surface of the wood finished smooth before cutting the letters. Parallel lines should be drawn across the panel the exact height of the letters and the correct spacing of the lines. Take a tracing of the first line of the inscription, cut a small portion at each end the exact height of the letters as a datum and attach to the wood at these points with adhesive tape. With a long line of letters it is advisable to check the centre and attach there also.

Trace the line of letters through to the wood using carbon paper; if the letters are small, it is only necessary to trace through the centre lines of the letter. When this is done, use a T square and set square and with a hard pencil mark in clearly the centre lines of all verticals; this will act as a guide to the chisel. For although there should be a certain amount of freedom in carved inscriptions, verticals should be truly vertical and not leaning to one side or the other.

Carving the letters

As with all carving, there should be a systematic approach to the work. With lettering, it is an advantage to do all the vertical strokes first and not to attempt to carve one letter at a time, which could involve the use of half a dozen tools. As in all carving, do all that is possible with the tool you have in your hand before changing it for another.

Choose a chisel a little shorter than the letter height, in order that the cut does not run into the serifs. As a beginner, do not use a chisel any wider than three quarters of an inch, or it will become difficult to control. Hold the tool vertically on the centre line and give it a sharp tap with the mallet. The purpose is to make a cut to the full depth of the letter; then with the chisel placed at the edge of the vertical and held at 60° to the work, again tap with the mallet and aim to reach to the full depth of the first cut. Repeat the operation from the opposite side of the vertical and the chip should come out clean (fig. 73).

With large letters and in hard woods it is not always possible to cut the letter to its full depth and width with

Fig. 75 Lettering with the parting tool. Pine.

the first cuts, so take it in two steps. When all the verticals are cut, continue in the same manner with the diagonals and lastly the horizontal strokes; these, being narrower than the uprights, should be shallower in depth, but before cutting them, first stab in the intersection of the planes of the serif. This will prevent the horizontals from splitting beyond the letter, as they are running in the direction of the grain of the wood.

For the curved shapes it is important that the gouges used should exactly fit the centre line of the letter. This may entail the use of two or three to produce a good flowing line, as in the case of the letter S. In cutting the V section of a curved letter, the same gouge can be used to chamfer the outside edge of the radius as for setting in; but for the opposite edge of the V, or inside of the letter, a flatter gouge is necessary, otherwise the corners will dig in. The widest part of a letter should be cut the deepest, getting gradually shallower as the width of the letter decreases.

To cut the serifs use the spade chisel. Lightly stab in the intersection of the planes, with the tool held at an angle to make the cut deepest at the point where the three planes meet; then with the chisel lying on one side of the V section of the vertical, continue the cut upward, gradually turning the tool through a radius as you approach the top and finishing on the line of intersection. Repeat this cut on the opposite side of the vertical, and finish by removing the chip at the top by cutting in the direction of the grain. This operation will not be difficult to students who have practised the chisel cuts described in the chapter on chip carving.

Another method of carving incised letters of large sizes, from three inches upwards in height, is to carve round the outline of the letter with a parting tool, and then make the body of the letter a shallow convex section. The serifs should be quite blunt. These letters are very suitable for painting or gilding.

Fig. 75 is an example of lettering out with one tool only, a parting tool. The inscription should be carefully drawn on the wood, and complete control over the tool is necessary. The best way of doing this is to use a light mallet, even though the wood may be soft. The hand holding the tool should rest firmly on the work or bench, and is used for guiding the tool round the drawing line while it is being given a series of short sharp taps with the mallet.

10 Inspiration

Not knowing what to carve is like an author not knowing what to write about. The best works of art are those whose subject matter is well within the reach of the artist, and reflects his desire to express the discoveries he has made about the life around him. It could be simple objects, or selections from the whole range of human, animal or insect life.

It is a good idea to attempt a copy of the work of a master, to discover how he translated his ideas into the material and to practise the technical problems that arise. All the great sculptors started in this way, but do not continue along this path. There are already too many Victorian copies of Roman reproductions of pieced together fragments of Greek originals, and in this lengthy process they have long since lost the spark of life given them by the original artist.

All forms in nature, whether plant life, animal or human, have their own individual characteristics; no two leaves are alike, but all leaves of one species conform to a similar pattern. This is true also of the growth of the bud, the stem and branch of a tree or plant, and it is not necessary to be close enough to see the shape of a leaf in order to distinguish one type of tree from another. It is this character and individual variation within the species that makes life interesting, and when an artist refers to nature for inspiration,

Fig. 76. Shaping a yew tree.

Fig. 77. Virgin and Child. South German, 16th century. (Reitlinger Bequest, Maidenhead, Berks, England.)

and at present there seems to be nothing better, it is most important that he should search out for this main feature or character of the subject. This should be apparent and contained in the finished work, whether it is representational or abstract, elaborate or simple, and the onlooker should be able to recognise and respond to this character, form or emotional content, as seen and depicted by the artist, whether he, the onlooker, understands or not how this effect has been achieved.

In order to discover this characteristic, it is necessary to observe nature more closely. If you see an animal grazing in a field, it is not enough just to recognise it as a cow, horse, or sheep. Try to look at things as if they have just appeared on earth for the first time; search with your eyes and brain every line, form, rhythm and growth from all angles. If the object or creature is stationary, walk around it, noticing how the profile is continually changing, offering new shapes and compositions at every turn.

There is a story or fable told about a Chinese Emperor who owned several hundred horses and spent many pleasant hours just watching them. One day a horse was attacked by an insect, and in the attempt to rid itself of the attacker, disported itself in so many intriguing attitudes that the Emperor decided he would like them recorded by his sculptor. Since that time, many copies of these have been reproduced in various mediums. The set I have illustrated in figs. 62 and 63 are carved in rosewood, are about two inches high, and come from Malaya.

In many cases it is the patron who decides the subject matter for the artist, and for centuries this was the church and its supporters. Some of the finest woodcarvings are to be found in the churches and cathedrals of Europe, with subjects from the Old and the New Testament in screens and altar pieces. Not so well known but worth seeking out are the misericords to be found on choir stalls not only in the abbeys and cathedrals but in many a village church. On lifting the seat you will discover on the underside a small shelf or corbel of just about the right height and size to act as a support during the long services, when standing was the rule. This is why it was called a mercy seat or misericord. The basic shape is almost always the same: a triangular composition below the shelf, acting as a support, and a circular motif on either side. But within this simple outline you can read the story of the people of those days; here they are depicted at work and play, musicians, carpenters and blacksmiths, singing, dancing, fighting, hunting, folk lore and fable, caricature and comment. The carvers were the cartoonists of their day, and more than one book would be needed to illustrate the great variety of subject matter to be found hidden away in these shadows.

In North America there are still a few remains of carving by a disappearing race of people who expressed in wood the story of the chiefs and ancestors of their tribes. These are the totem poles of the Indians, carved from great cedar trees of up to a height of fifty feet or more, and incorporating human and animal forms, scrolls and symbols, which can be translated by those who know their history. These also are a kind of strip cartoon, and are read from the top downwards.

Simplification of form and elimination of detail in order to emphasise the basic theme or interpretation of a subject will gradually lead to the non-representational or abstract form, where the subject matter has disappeared and only shapes remain. These can conjure up in the mind of the onlooker innumerable impressions related only to his own personal experiences and observations.

In fig. 68, a and c are examples which could be regarded as being in the transitional stage between representational and abstract.

Fig. 78 Oak chest with raised lettering. (Victoria and Albert Museum. Crown copyright.)

For further reading

Wood Carving by Alan Durst. Studio Publications, London and New York, 1961.

Minor English Wood Sculpture 1400-1550 by A. Gardner. A. Tiranti, London, 1958.

Bird Carving by Wendell Gilley. D. Van Nostrand, New York, London, Toronto, 1961.

Grinling Gibbons by David Green. Country Life, London, 1965.

Principles of Woodworking by Holstrop & Hjorth. The Bruce Publishing Co., Milwaukee, Wisconsin, 1961.

Creative Wood Craft by Ernst Rottger. Batsford, London, 1961. Published as Creative Wood Design by Reinhold, New York, 1963.

Woodworking for Everybody by John G. Shea. D. Van Nostrand, New York, London, Toronto, 3rd edition 1961.

Human Anatomy for Art Students by S. Tresilian and H. Williams. Chapman & Hall, London, 1961.

Whittling and Woodcarving by E. J. Tangerman. Dover Publications, New York, 1936.

List of suppliers

Ashley Iles (edge tools) Ltd, Pensylvia Works, Solly St, Sheffield 1. Manufacturers and suppliers.

W. Marples & Sons Ltd, Sheffield. Manufacturers, supplied through agents.

Henry Taylor, Woodside Works, Rutland Rd, Sheffield 3. Manufacturers, supplied through agents.

Alec Tiranti Ltd, 72 Charlotte St, London, W.1.

U.S. suppliers

Albert Constantine & Sons, Inc., 2050 Teastchester Rd, New York. Imported and domestic woods and veneers; woodworking tools and equipment. Write for catalog.

Craftsman Wood Service, 2727 South Mary St, Chicago, Illinois. Domestic and exotic woods, both veneers and lumber; all wood-working tools, including imported. Excellent catalog.

H. L. Wild, 510 East 11th St, New York. Comprehensive stock of rare and exotic woods and veneers; interesting line of tools.

Woodcraft Supply Co., 71 Canal St, Boston, Mass. Woods, domestic and exotic; comprehensive list of tools. Catalog.

Index